The Fairy Party

Cataloging in Publication
Clibbon, Meg
The fairy party book / Magic Meg, Lucy Loveheart.
ISBN 1-55037-914-3
1. Children's parties—Juvenile literature.   2. Fairies—
Juvenile literature.   I. Clibbon, Lucy   II. Title.
GV1205.C55 2005   j793.2'1   C2005-901405-9

Distributed in Canada and the U.S.A. by Firefly Books Ltd.
www.annickpress.com
Printed and bound in China

The Fairy Party Book

Magic Meg
and
Lucy Loveheart

for Rachel and Amie,
our special fairy friends

Annick Press Ltd.
Toronto • New York • Vancouver

Introduction

Magic Meg and Lucy Loveheart have been visiting the Enchanted Forest to find out how fairies celebrate. Now they can let you into some of the secrets of fairy parties – how they plan the great occasions, what they like to wear, the food they eat, the games they play and lots more. Of course, the fairies won't mind if you copy some of their ideas for your own parties.

Have fun!

Fairies and Parties

Fairies are usually busy all day long. There are always jobs to do
in the Enchanted Forest: polishing toadstools, collecting flower petals,
working in the fairy dust factory, and mending wands and wings.
After all this work the fairies often like to unwind with a party.
Fairies are party creatures at heart and they are nearly always happy.
They have a special gift for making other people happy too,
and a good way to do this is to have a party.

A party can be for any reason: a new baby fairy, a midsummer festival, moving to a new toadstool, a birthday, starting on a journey, planting a new garden, spotting a shooting star, or just about anything.

There are different types of parties, of course, and part of the excitement is the planning and thinking of how everyone can enjoy themselves. All the fairies help, so everyone has fun and that is what parties are all about.

Planning a Party

When the fairies have decided to have a party they hold a meeting, and because they are fairies this meeting turns into a party too – a planning party. They make themselves comfortable on a ring of dandelion heads, armed with a notebook and pencil, a glass of fizzy flower juice, and a fairy cake. Then they start to think – it is amazing how a notebook and pencil and something to eat and drink can help you to think. When the ideas come bursting out, lists are made, everyone is given a job and hurries off to make a start. Isn't it infuriating when someone is given a job and doesn't do it? This never happens at fairy planning parties because they know that hard work and team work equals fun, fun, fun.

Get your friends together with a small snack and plan a party involving everyone. It could be for a birthday, moving house, a new pet, or just about anything.

Party Themes

Some parties celebrate a special event and these parties have their own theme, but whenever they can, the fairies dream and scheme of themes and scenes which are quite different and quite magical. Imagine, for example, an early morning bluebell party with everyone dressed in shades of blue, dancing under the beech trees and then enjoying a party breakfast of fried beech nuts and wild garlic.

Fairies never run out of ideas for parties. Here are some of their favorites:

Masked Ball
Sparkling eyes peep out from pretty decorated masks.

Fancy Dress
A good opportunity for fairies to dress up as all sorts of things.

Flower Party
Fairies love flowers and flowers love fairies so why not have a party?

Sleepover
Nobody is very sleepy at a sleeopver party, of course!

Invitations and Guests

The trickiest part about organizing any party is deciding who to invite. Do you remember the trouble that was caused at the palace when the wicked fairy was not invited to Sleeping Beauty's christening party? Nobody wants to risk that sort of catastrophe.

When the list of guests is ready, the invitations must be made and sent out in plenty of time. The artist fairies have lovely workrooms full of glitter, birch bark, special hand-made paper, and lots of helpers who check that the date, time, place, and theme are clearly written. Then the invitations are given to the robin post and the guests can start to get ready.

Design a card with a pretty border and make enough copies for your party invitations. Then write in the important details on each one.

You are invited to
_____ party
on
_____
at
_____
please reply to
_____

Food and Drink

A party just isn't a party without food and drink. Fairies love making food, displaying it beautifully – and then eating it!

While the pixies gather berries and edible flowers, the gnomes search in the tree roots and under fern leaves for mushrooms, and water nymphs draw cool water from the spring to make sparkling cordials. When everything is collected, the mixing and straining and stirring begin.

In the center of everything is Gordon the Goblin, whose job is to make the Fairy Queen's favorite cake, with dates and walnuts and toffee topping. His kitchen below the Scots pine is hot and fiery but when he emerges with the cake the scene is set. Fragrant smells fill the woody glade and as the fairies begin to gather, the elves and nymphs pass baskets of marshmallows and goblets brimming over with foaming fruit juices.

Pass the Party Parcel

Tiny presents, one for every guest, are wrapped in gossamer and then wrapped into one big parcel with many layers of wrapping. The parcel is passed from one fairy to another. When the music stops, the fairy holding the parcel takes off one layer and the game continues until there are no more layers. In the middle there is a prize for every fairy.

Musical Mushrooms

The fairies dance and fly about until the music stops and they all have to find a mushroom to sit on. One mushroom is removed each turn. This usually results in fairies sitting on each other and rolling off the toadstools in great merriment.

Fairy Godmother's Footsteps

The Fairy Godmother turns her back and all the little fairies creep up to her quietly. If she turns round and spots them moving, they are out.

Feathers

The fairies lie perfectly still in the dancing ring. Two of them go round with feathers tickling the others. Those who laugh are out. Of course they can't stop themselves laughing so at the end of the game the dancing ring is full of giggling fairies.

Dizzy Pixie

Pixies chase fairies until they are all caught and then they change over and fairies chase pixies. This game is exhausting and they all get dizzy. The pixies usually win.

Music and Dancing

The Enchanted Forest is full of music: trickling streams and gushing waterfalls, rustling leaves, flower bells tinkling, the breeze swishing through grasses and ferns, birds calling and little animals whispering to each other. At night a dreamy sound seems to drift down from the stars and planets. When fairies give parties there is also music for dancing and playing. You cannot stand still to this music. Something seems to nibble your toes so that you want to dance and hop and fly about. The main music fairy is a sprite with sparkling eyes and a high-tech mushroom which sends out music to make the dancing ring hum with excitement. Then the fun begins and the fairies dance and fly and dance again until they are tired out, happy and, of course, terribly fit because dancing is such good exercise.

Make your own fairy music with a wind chime made out of shells or other natural objects. Hang it by the door or in an open window and let the breeze do the rest.

Decorations

Decorations help to create the right atmosphere at parties. Fairies plan their decorations to please the five senses of sight, sound, smell, touch, and taste.

For an outdoor party, make star templates and spray star shapes on to the grass with paint or glitter. (These will grow out later.) Indoors, hang stars of silver foil on pretty ribbons.

Everywhere there are pretty things to look at, pleasing sounds, fragrant perfumes, silky textures, and tasty morsels.

Dressing Up

Parties are the perfect excuse to dress up. Fairies have lots of fun dressing up for parties and take great delight in…

| Face painting | Masks | Headdresses | Make-up |
| Wigs | Hats | Jewellery | Gloves |

Ask your party guests to each choose a different color to wear. When they all arrive it will be a living rainbow. Rainbow iced cakes and different colored drinks and decorations will complete the effect.

Fairy Tea Party

Every day in the Enchanted Forest there is an opportunity for an afternoon party because every day the fairies have tea. It could be a picnic on a rug of knitted thistledown, or a jolly tea party deep in the roots of an underground tree house. Wherever the fairies have tea there are cakes: frosty cakes with crunchy bits, light spongy cakes that melt in the mouth, and toffee cakes with chocolate topping. They are all beautifully decorated and the fairies love making them as well as eating them.

Fairy Party Cake

You will need:

1/2 cup butter

6 tablespoons cocoa powder

2 tablespoons evaporated milk

1/2 cup superfine or
   granulated sugar

1 tablespoon golden syrup

8 oz. package of tea biscuits

2 tablespoons candied
   cherries, chopped

2 tablespoons walnuts,
   chopped (optional)

1/4 cup chocolate chips

What to do:

Warm the butter. Break the biscuits into small pieces inside
a plastic bag, using a rolling pin. Blend all the ingredients
together and press into a cake pan with a loose bottom.
Leave the pan in the refrigerator overnight to chill. Turn
out the cake and use your imagination to decorate the cake
beautifully with pretty things that are good to eat.

Evening Fairy Party

Since larkrise, the busy pixies and elves have been
baking chestnut cakes, fairy bars, and chocolate logs.
Elderflower cordial is cooling in the spring, and the birchwood
barbecue is beginning to glow red hot. Now the fairies
are polishing the tops of the toadstools and placing them
in the fairy ring. The porcupines have made themselves
into prickly balls and are rolling around the dancing green
to gather up fallen leaves and moss.
The spiders are spinning silvery gossamer garlands
to hang from the trees, and all around the tree roots
the glow worms make little fiery corners.
As dusk falls, these little glowing lights shine on
the gossamer and the fairy dust, and when the moon and
stars come out to take a look, the fairy dell is sparkling
and twinkling and ready for the party to begin.

There's lots of magic in these books!

1-55037-914-3 pbk

1-55037-791-4 hbk
1-55037-790-6 pbk

1-55037-793-0 hbk
1-55037-792-2 pbk

1-55037-743-4 hbk
1-55037-742-6 pbk

1-55037-741-8 hbk
1-55037-740-X pbk

1-55037-921-6 hbk
1-55037-920-8 pbk

1-55037-919-4 hbk
1-55037-918-6 pbk